Sweets

IN THE RAW

NATURALLY HEALTHY DESSERTS

LAURA MARQUIS

NATURALLY HEALTHY
Est. DESSERTS 2015
· organic ·

Naturally Healthy Desserts
10425 Tierrasanta Blvd 102
San Diego, CA 92124
www.naturallyhealthydesserts.com

Cover photo by Mike Carpenter
Interior photography by Mike Carpenter and Paulina LaScola

Cover and Interior design by Stacey Uy
Indexing by Laura Marquis

ISBN: 978-0-9971048-0-6

LCCN: 2015920739

Printed in China by Global PSD

THIS BOOK IS DEDICATED TO

My husband, best friend and taste tester who has been there for me every step of the way! Dan, I would not be living my dreams without all of your love and support. You make every day of my life just a little sweeter!

My Mom and Dad who inspired me to be the person I am today! You both helped me believe that the only person who could ever stop me was myself! That gift is priceless. Thank you!

And last but not least, many thanks to all the people in my life who have encouraged me to not only dream, but to chase my dreams!

Table of Contents

CHAPTER 1
Essentials

CHAPTER 2
Bars, Bites & Cookies

CHAPTER 3
Cakes & Tarts

CHAPTER 4
Candies, Fudge & Truffles

CHAPTER 5
Frozen Treats, Ice Cream & Sorbet

Why Naturally Healthy Desserts?

Why Naturally Healthy Desserts? They are my secret weapon for success in living a Naturally Healthy Lifestyle every day, and now they can be yours too.

Desserts are my weakness. Not only because I love a sweet treat, but because I cherish the ritual of preparing and serving desserts. I enjoy seeing the face of a loved one light up with a smile after that first bite. For a long time now I have been on a journey to discover a more healthful answer to the question, "What's for dessert?"

When I was a little girl, I spent countless hours playing in the kitchen while my mom made wedding cakes and delicious homemade desserts. But the treats that I enjoyed, like cake and frosting, made me feel so physically sick that I had to lie down while my sisters went outside to play, energized by their sugar high. Soon, other foods like pizza, sandwiches, cereal and yogurt made me so incredibly ill that I refused to eat them. My mom tried really hard to understand why my sisters could eat "regular" food and feel fine, but not me. I was in a constant conflict with my heart for many years—wanting to enjoy my mom's homemade desserts, but knowing my body would always suffer for it.

Twenty years later, I finally learned that I am gluten and lactose intolerant. Initially, having to radically change my diet felt very isolating because my friends and family couldn't understand why I wouldn't "just have a bite" of the dessert they wanted to share. I wasn't trying to deprive myself of pleasure, I was trying to avoid feeling sick!

Then one day a client at Marquis Pilates introduced me to raw desserts. When I first tasted the raw brownie that my client had prepared for me, I thought, "This is it! I can finally enjoy dessert again!" I couldn't believe how easy the dessert was to make once she shared the recipe! I realized that this was a way for my clients and me to still eat healthy, and indulge in dessert without feeling ill or deprived. But, when I began trying new raw dessert recipes, I found that many didn't taste right. They just weren't satisfying enough to completely replace the flavors and textures of traditional desserts. My mother had taught me the importance of quality in homemade desserts, and that was not something that I wanted to compromise.

I made it my mission to create the very first raw dessert cookbook that meets the dessert lover's expectations for taste and quality, but without using any refined sugar. This was no small feat! After years of playing in my kitchen, using my husband as my personal taste-testing guinea pig and never settling for "good enough" results, I am so happy to share my Naturally Healthy Desserts with you.

With Love,

Laura Marquis

Naturally Healthy at a Glance

Naturally Healthy Desserts can be enjoyed regularly without all the negative side effects that come with traditional desserts. Each carefully crafted recipe will naturally satisfy a craving for sweets without compromising the flavor and texture expected from a decadent dessert. Naturally Healthy Desserts are also the best option available to support your healthy lifestyle because:

☑ **ALL DESSERTS ARE RAW!** Most of us will never become full-time raw foodies, but that doesn't mean that we can't enjoy the benefits of raw food with desserts! There is no sweeter way to get your enzymes, vitamins, minerals and fiber!

☑ **WHOLE INGREDIENTS ONLY.** My recipes include easy to find, minimally processed foods like raw nuts, fruits and spices.

☑ **MADE FROM SCRATCH.** Naturally Healthy Desserts are homemade and handcrafted which means no fake or artificial ingredients!

☑ **NO REFINED SUGAR!** I believe everything in moderation is okay, with the exception of REFINED SUGAR! You will never see "healthy" refined sugars in my recipes such as organic sugar, agave or maple syrup because of what these refined sugars do to your waistline and to your health.

☑ **NO GLUTEN OR WHEAT!** With gluten intolerance and wheat allergies on the rise, there is no reason to include these potentially inflammatory ingredients in my desserts. I do not use any ingredients that contain gluten or refined grains!

☑ **NO DAIRY!** Dairy is NOT a super food! Most people only consume dairy that has been pasteurized. During that process, vitamins, proteins and enzymes are destroyed, decreasing the nutritional value. My recipes focus on only using great quality ingredients that nourish and heal the whole body!

☑ **TESTED AND APPROVED!** Hours, days and sometimes weeks were spent perfecting these recipes so that you can enjoy the best possible Naturally Healthy Dessert. Each and every recipe passed numerous taste tests, by adults and kids alike, with flying colors.

☑ **EASY TO MAKE.** I don't use a lot of equipment, so most of my desserts can be made by simply using a good blender and food processor.

The Truth About Sugar

We all know sugar isn't great for us. We know sugar is linked to diseases like type 2 diabetes and weight gain, yet for some reason we continue to eat it. Is it because of the sweet, satisfying flavor? Is it because consuming sweet treats brings us back to a time when we baked cookies with our mom or grandma? Actually, research shows that we are ADDICTED to sugar! The more we eat sugar, the more we want sugar! The fact that it is a hidden ingredient in almost everything means that it's hard to avoid.

The other tricky part about trying to reduce or eliminate sugar is that it is unclear what kind of sugar is okay for us to eat. To simplify this, I only use minimally processed, natural sweeteners with fiber that create little to no blood sugar spike. The only natural sugar sources that you will find in this recipe book are dried fruit and yacon syrup. And most recipes will have less than 1 date worth of sugar per serving.

Sweeteners that will not be used due to their negative impact on health include:

- Agave
- Brown Rice Syrup
- Beet Sugar
- Organic Sugar Cane
- Raw Sugar
- Maple Syrup
- Turbinado Sugar
- Fruit Juice

WHAT IS YACON SYRUP?

So what is yacon syrup, and why should you use it instead of the other so-called "healthy" sugars? Well, because it is actually healthy! Yacon syrup is an extract from the root of the South American yacon plant with a color and flavor similar to molasses. Yacon syrup is high in antioxidants, very low on the glycemic index and has recently been classified as a superfood!

NATURAL SWEETENER	GLYCEMIC LOAD
Yacon Syrup	1
Agave	15
Brown Rice Syrup	25
Coconut Palm Sugar	35
Organic Cane Juice	43
Honey	50
Maple Syrup	54
Blackstrap Molasses	55

TIPS & TRICKS

READ THE ENTIRE RECIPE BEFORE STARTING & USE THE ICONS

There is nothing worse than starting a recipe and realizing you don't have an ingredient on hand or that you were supposed to have soaked or melted an ingredient first. To maximize your time and ensure the quality of your dessert, you will find icons at the top of every recipe that will allow you to see what is required for soak prep and freeze time.

QUALITY OVER QUANTITY

I learned this one the hard way! When I started creating the recipes in this book, I tried looking for ingredients that cost less to save a little money. But I found that the taste and quality of the dessert made with cheaper ingredients suffered. The truth is that the fresher your ingredients, the better every recipe will taste...especially with nuts. Rancid (old) nuts will change the flavor of everything. So be picky and only get the best!

WHERE TO FIND QUALITY INGREDIENTS

I am a huge lover of local ingredients, and I regularly get all of my produce from farmers markets and Whole Foods. But if those places aren't available near you, try buying seasonal fruit at your local grocery store. If you want to make a specific dessert but the fruit is out of season, simply buy the frozen option. Fruit is usually frozen at its freshest, right after

harvest. As for coconut oil, nut butters and yacon syrup, I suggest buying them online if they are not available at your supermarket.

TASTE ALONG THE WAY

It seems like I always go through half of my silverware drawer every time I make a dessert, using spoons to sample everything because I want it to be perfect. Make sure you always taste everything: crust, filling, topping and the fruit. We are using fresh ingredients that vary in flavor, so my recipes could come out slightly different each time. Decide if you would like it to taste a little sweeter, saltier or more chocolaty! These desserts are for you and your friends and family so they should taste exactly how you want!

REFINED COCONUT OIL VS UNREFINED COCONUT OIL

You will see that some recipes call for coconut oil and some recipes call for refined coconut oil. This is very important as there is a noticeable flavor difference between the two! Refined coconut oil has little to no coconut flavor, whereas the unrefined, or virgin, coconut oil packs a big punch of coconut flavor.

TIPS & TRICKS (CONTINUED)

COCONUT OIL VS COCONUT BUTTER

Coconut oil is simply the oil that is extracted from the meat of a coconut. Coconut butter is a creamy purée of coconut meat. They cannot be interchanged without significantly changing the recipe. Always make sure you stir the coconut butter before using as the oil separates and rises to the top.

HOW TO LIQUEFY COCONUT OILS AND COCONUT BUTTERS

Place the amount of coconut oil or butter needed into a glass jar or bowl. Set that into a larger bowl of hot water. Let sit until completely melted.

PROPER STORAGE FOR DESSERTS

I know it is hard to believe, but if there should happen to be any leftovers, I suggest storing them in a freezer-safe container to lock-in and maintain freshness.

HELPFUL MEASUREMENTS

CUP	FL OZ	TBSP	TSP	ML
1 C	8 oz	16 tbsp	48 tsp	237 mL
¾ C	6 oz	12 tbsp	36 tsp	177 mL
⅔ C	5⅓ oz	10.6 tbsp	32 tsp	158 mL
½ C	4 oz	8 tbsp	24 tsp	118 mL
⅓ C	2⅔ oz	5.3 tbsp	16 tsp	79 mL
¼ C	2 oz	4 tbsp	12 tsp	59 mL
⅛ C	1 oz	2 tbsp	6 tsp	30 mL
1/16 C	½ oz	1 tbsp	3 tsp	15 mL

Equipment

FOOD PROCESSOR

The food processor is a fundamental piece of equipment when preparing raw desserts, because it will perfectly break down the ingredients. It's also important to note that every food processor works a little differently. I personally went through four food processors before I found the model that I liked. For the perfect texture in every dessert I highly suggest using the *Breville Model BFP660*. You may use another brand but please keep in mind that it may alter the consistency of the recipe.

HIGH SPEED BLENDER

The high speed blender is also a very important piece of equipment. The two most common brands are *Blendtec* and *Vitamix*. This will be the most expensive piece of equipment required. You can start with the blender that you already have, but you may find that the resulting textures are too chunky.

SPRINGFORM PAN & SILICONE MOLDS

I highly suggest using a springform pan or silicone mold for cheesecake recipes. They help give a perfect shape to your desserts, but they are not required. If this isn't something you have readily available then simply line the bottom of any pan with parchment paper.

When using a springform pan, be sure to firmly press the bottom crust layer into the pan to ensure the bottom crust stays intact when you remove the base. It also helps to first use a warm cloth to remove the frost from the sides of the pan. To remove the dessert, unlatch the clasp, and you should easily be able to slide the ring mold off. Then use a serving spatula to remove the cake from the base of the pan.

As for the silicone molds, simply pop the dessert out by flipping the mold inside out.

ICE CREAM MAKER

This is something I recommend, but it is not required. You can make the recipes in this book without one, but please note that when you freeze the ice cream mixture it will become very hard and dense. I have three recipes that call for an ice cream maker, and if you really like ice cream, then you will use these recipes often enough to invest in one. I personally love the *Cuisinart Sorbet & Ice Cream Maker*.

CHAPTER 1
ESSENTIALS

Sweet Almond Milk

Store-bought almond milk just isn't my thing, but this homemade version is D-E-L-I-C-I-O-U-S! I first created it for my mom to use in her coffee, but now I use it in almost everything!

INGREDIENTS

- 1 cup almonds (soaked overnight)
- 6 medjool dates
- ½ teaspoon vanilla extract
- 1 vanilla bean pod (optional)
- dash of salt
- 5 cups water
- ⅛ teaspoon cinnamon

HOW TO MAKE

Place all ingredients in a blender, and blend for 2 minutes. Strain through a nut milk bag, cheesecloth or mesh strainer bowl. Serve and enjoy, or seal in airtight mason jars in the refrigerator for up to 7 days.

Helpful Hints

If you use a nut milk bag or cheesecloth, be sure to squeeze out all the remaining liquid from the nut milk to make the cleaning process easier.

Sweet Cashew Milk

If I only knew how easy it was to make non-dairy milk, I would have started making it a long time ago. I drink this luscious milk on days I don't have time for breakfast and add it to smoothies and any dessert that calls for milk.

INGREDIENTS

- ½ cup raw cashews (soaked for 2 hours)
- 5 medjool dates
- ½ teaspoon vanilla extract
- 1 vanilla bean pod, scraped (optional)
- 3 cups water
- ⅛ teaspoon cinnamon
- ⅛ teaspoon nutmeg
- dash of salt

HOW TO MAKE

Place all ingredients in a blender and blend for 2 minutes. Serve and enjoy, or seal in airtight mason jars in the refrigerator for up to 7 days.

 Helpful Hints

A little nutmeg and cinnamon in this drink go a long way, so use sparingly.

Cashew Milk

Cold Brew Coffee

Are you a coffee lover? Cold brew coffee is so easy to make! This method decreases the acidity level and bitter flavor that hot brew coffee can sometimes have. Not to mention it carries a powerful punch.

INGREDIENTS

- 1 cup organic ground coffee
- 4 cups water

HOW TO MAKE

Place the ground coffee into a large glass bowl, and then add the water. Briefly stir the coffee mixture, cover and refrigerate for 12 hours. Strain out the coffee grounds using a nut milk bag, cheesecloth or mesh strainer bowl. Discard the coffee grounds. Store cold brew coffee in a mason jar, or other glass container with an airtight lid, in the refrigerate for up to 7 days.

Helpful Hints

I don't just use this recipe for my desserts, I also pair this cold brew coffee with the Sweet Almond Milk recipe to make my favorite pick-me-up beverage!

Chocolate Sauce

A fresh batch of this chocolate sauce is perfect for straight-up chocolate lovers! I love dipping fruit in it, or drizzling it over my favorite desserts! You will find this yumminess starring in several other recipes throughout the book.

INGREDIENTS

- ¼ cup refined coconut oil, melted
- ½ teaspoon vanilla extract
- 3 tablespoons yacon syrup
- ¼ cup cacao powder

HOW TO MAKE

Mix all wet ingredients together in a small mixing bowl. Add cacao powder and whisk until well blended. Use on anything that requires chocolaty goodness!

 Helpful Hints

*It is **crucial** that you mix all wet ingredients and then add in the cacao powder. If you do this out of order, your chocolate will turn out chunky.*

Date Paste

Dates are sweet and full of fiber which makes them one of my favorite natural sweeteners. Be sure to note this basic recipe as it will be featured in many other raw desserts later in the book.

INGREDIENTS

- 2 cups lightly packed medjool dates
- ½ cup water
- ½ teaspoon vanilla extract

HOW TO MAKE

Blend all ingredients in the blender until smooth and creamy.

Helpful Hints

This recipe can be stored in your refrigerator for 2 weeks or the freezer for up to a month. If you do store Date Paste in the freezer, be sure to give it time to thaw before adding it your recipes.

Coconut Vanilla Whipped Cream

This is the perfect topping for almost any dessert! This whipped cream has a slight hint of coconut and vanilla flavor.

INGREDIENTS

- 1 can of coconut cream, chilled overnight
- 1 teaspoon vanilla extract
- 2 teaspoons Date Paste (see Essentials)

HOW TO MAKE

Scoop out the firm coconut cream from the top half of the can. Discard remaining liquid. Mix with electric mixer until light and fluffy. The whipped cream can last for up to 1 week in the refrigerator.

 Helpful Hints

Don't prepare the whipped cream until you are ready to serve, as it does not hold its shape as well as traditional whipped cream.

CHAPTER 2

BARS, BITES & COOKIES

Cherry Strudel

Sometimes there are no words to describe how amazing something actually tastes! This recipe took me a couple tries to nail, but it is one of my all-time favorites! With a burst of fruit flavor, and a light hint of cinnamon and pecan, this dessert will have your friends and family begging for more!

INGREDIENTS

Base Layer

- 1 cup unsweetened shredded coconut
- ½ cup raw cashews
- dash of salt
- 2 teaspoons Date Paste (see Essentials)

Fruit Layer

- 1 ½ cup cherries (or fruit of choice)
- 1 tablespoon Date Paste (see Essentials)
- 1 tablespoon refined coconut oil, warmed

Crumble Layer

- ½ cup pecans
- 3 medjool dates
- ¼ teaspoon cinnamon
- ¼ teaspoon vanilla extract
- dash of salt

HOW TO MAKE

Base Layer

Process coconut, cashews and salt until a flour-like consistency in the food processor. Add Date Paste to the mixture and continue processing until everything is evenly mixed. Press crust firmly into a 4x4 inch pan lined with parchment paper. Set aside.

Fruit Layer

Blend all ingredients in the blender until smooth. Evenly spread over the base layer. Place in the refrigerator.

Crumble Layer

Process all ingredients in the food processor until you see an even chunky crumble. Sprinkle on fruit layer. Freeze for 1 hour, then cut and serve. Uneaten dessert can be stored in the refrigerator for up to 1 week or in the freezer for up to 1 month.

Helpful Hints

If you plan to serve these delicious treats to guests and want them to look perfect, freeze for 2 hours and cut while still frozen with a warm knife. This will ensure you don't have to deal with misshapen bars or messy crumbles. This is also one of the few recipes that requires fresh fruit! Frozen fruit will leave your dessert looking runny.

Chocolate Chip Cookie Dough

The feedback I received from these chocolate chip cookies was what inspired me to create my very own raw dessert cookbook! I brought these little guys to an open house I was hosting for my studio and EVERYONE loved them! This recipe is a great way to dip your toe into the sweet world of raw desserts!

INGREDIENTS

- ¼ cup pecans
- ¼ cup walnuts
- ⅔ cup deglet noor dates
- ¼ teaspoon vanilla extract
- pinch of salt
- handful of chocolate cut into tiny chunks (see Chocolate Bar recipe)

HOW TO MAKE

Process all ingredients except for chocolate chunks in the food processor until the dough turns into small one inch balls. Sprinkle in chocolate chunks and pulse. Roll into a ball first, then press flat into the shape of a cookie. Serve and enjoy. Uneaten dessert can be stored in the refrigerator for up to 1 week.

Helpful Hints

Hand-shaping or rolling these little bites of joy are typically how I serve these treats, but if you would like to step it up a notch use two sheets of parchment paper. (One sheet under the dough and one over the top to ensure no mess.) Roll them out with rolling pin. Remove the top piece of parchment, then cut with your cookie cutter of choice!

Dark Chocolate Fudge Brownies

If you are looking for the perfect marriage of rich and chocolaty, this is your match! A raw brownie was the very first raw dessert I ever had! After one bite I fell in love and I have never looked back!

INGREDIENTS

- 1 cup walnuts
- 1 ⅓ cup deglet noor dates
- 1 teaspoon vanilla extract
- 4 tablespoons cacao powder
- ⅛ teaspoon salt

HOW TO MAKE

Process all ingredients in the food processor until finely ground and well combined. It will look crumbly in consistency, but should hold together when you pinch the mixture together in your hands. Line a 4x4 inch pan with parchment paper, then press the mixture firmly into the pan or roll into small one inch balls. Serve and enjoy. Uneaten dessert can be stored in the refrigerator for up to 1 week.

 ## Helpful Hints

Be careful not to over process the ingredients. You will want to process just long enough so that when you squeeze the mixture firmly it should hold together. You will know you have over processed if the mixture seems excessively oily.

Lemon Frosted Cookies

These little bites of sunshine are really something special. I created these treats for my Grandma and Grandpa Cunningham who love anything with lemon. They are the perfect blend of sweet and tart.

INGREDIENTS

Cookie Layer

- 1 cup unsweetened shredded coconut
- 1 cup raw cashews
- pinch of salt
- 3 tablespoons Date Paste (see Essentials)
- 1 teaspoon vanilla extract
- 1 teaspoon lemon zest

Frosting Layer

- ¼ cup coconut butter, warmed (mixed)
- ½ lemon juiced
- 1 tablespoon Date Paste (see Essentials)
- 2 teaspoons lemon zest

HOW TO MAKE

Cookie Layer

Process all dry ingredients in the food processor until flour-like in consistency. Add all wet ingredients and process until the dough turns into ball. Set the dough in the refrigerator for 20 minutes or until dough is firm. Once firm, use parchment paper to roll the dough out and cut into cookies.

Frosting Layer

Whisk all ingredients, except 1 teaspoon lemon zest, together in a small bowl. Frost cookies. Sprinkle with reserved lemon zest for decoration. Serve and enjoy! Uneaten dessert can be stored in the refrigerator for up to 1 week.

Helpful Hints

I like to make these cookies and store them in the refrigerator in a tupperware container 1-2 days before I plan on enjoying them. This improves the texture of the cookie. I also suggest not sprinkling lemon zest onto your cookies until you get ready to serve as the zest dries out rather quickly.

Chocolate Macaroons

I was never much of a coconut lover until I combined it with chocolate. Now I can't get enough! The combination is magic. These macaroons have just the right amount of chocolate to complement the coconut perfectly!

INGREDIENTS

- 1 ½ cup unsweetened shredded coconut
- 2 teaspoon cacao powder
- 1 tablespoon coconut oil, warmed
- 1 tablespoon Date Paste (see Essentials)
- ½ teaspoon vanilla extract
- dash of salt

HOW TO MAKE

Pulse all ingredients in food processor until well combined but still chunky. Use a mini ice cream scoop to create small bite-size desserts. Set onto parchment paper onto plate. Refrigerate for 10 minutes or until firm. Serve and enjoy. Uneaten dessert can be stored in the refrigerator for up to 1 week.

Helpful Hints

To make these macaroons pop just a little more, top them off with a drizzle of fresh chocolate. (see Chocolate Sauce recipe)

PREP

8 min

Peanut Butter Cookies

Creating these raw peanut butter cookies brought me back in time to when I was a little girl baking with my mom. She is the one who taught me how to make my first batch of cookies, and I can't thank her enough! These cookies are soft, moist and will fully satisfy your peanut butter craving!

INGREDIENTS

- ½ cup natural peanut butter
- ¾ cup raisins
- ¼ cup peanuts
- ¼ teaspoon vanilla extract
- dash of salt

HOW TO MAKE

Process all ingredients in the food processor until well combined. Consistency will look crumbly but should hold together when you pinch the mixture together in your hands. Roll into a ball first, then press flat into the shape of a cookie. Then, score the top of each cookie with a fork. Serve and enjoy. Uneaten dessert can be stored in the refrigerator for up to 1 week.

Helpful Hints

To make the perfect score mark on each cookie, press your dough into little coin shapes and then score once top to bottom and then once left to right.

Orange Zest Brownie Bites

I am taking brownies to the next level with a burst of orange! These bites of yumminess are so good that they never last in my house for longer than 24 hours! Go ahead and try this fresh take on brownies, but don't say I didn't warn you when they become your new obsession.

INGREDIENTS

- 1 cup walnuts
- 1 ⅓ cup deglet noor dates
- 1 teaspoon vanilla extract
- 4 tablespoons cacao powder
- ⅛ teaspoon salt
- ½ a fresh orange, juiced
- 1 tablespoon orange zest

HOW TO MAKE

Process all ingredients, except for orange juice, in the food processor until finely ground. Consistency will look crumbly but should hold together when you pinch the mixture together in your hands. Add juice and pulse until well blended. Roll into bite size balls. Serve and enjoy. Uneaten dessert can be stored in the refrigerator for up to 1 week.

 Helpful Hints

Keep these brownie bites in an airtight container or bag to ensure the same softness and chewiness days later.

Vanilla Bean Macaroons

These raw macaroons are made for anyone with a slightly more refined palate. With a hint of sweetness and a beautiful aroma of coconut and vanilla, these treats will make any coconut lover's dream come true!

INGREDIENTS

- 1 ½ cup unsweetened shredded coconut
- 1 tablespoon coconut oil, warmed
- 1 tablespoon Date Paste (see Essentials)
- 1 vanilla bean pod, scraped
- dash of salt

HOW TO MAKE

Process all ingredients in the food processor until well combined but still chunky. Use a small ice cream scoop to create small, bite-size scoops. Place them onto a small plate and refrigerate for 10 minutes. Serve and enjoy. Uneaten dessert can be stored in the refrigerator for up to 1 week.

Helpful Hints

Try coating the macaroons in chocolate (see Chocolate Sauce recipe) for an extraordinary finish.

Oatmeal Raisin Cookies

Oatmeal raisin cookies are special treats that will never go out of style. For that very reason, I have created a recipe that is great for "big kids" like you and me, as well as little ones. With the sweetness from the dates, the chunky texture from the walnuts and oats, and the hint of cinnamon flavor these things are just so darn good!

INGREDIENTS

- ¾ cup walnuts
- ½ cup gluten-free oats
- ½ cup raisins
- ½ cup dates
- 1 vanilla bean pod, scraped
- 2 teaspoons cinnamon
- pinch of salt
- ¼ cup raisins or chocolate chunks (optional)

HOW TO MAKE

Process all ingredients, except for the optional raisins/chocolate chunks, in a food processor until well combined, but still chunky. Mix in raisins or chocolate chunks, shape into cookies, serve and enjoy. Uneaten dessert can be stored in the refrigerator or at room temperature for up to 1 week.

 Helpful Hints

If you would like the cookies to be a little sweeter, substitute the vanilla bean for 1 teaspoon of vanilla extract.

SOAK

2 hrs

PREP

15 min

FREEZE

1 hr

Fig Bars

If you like Fig Newtons, then meet your healthy, no-guilt option! The filling is a perfect blend of orange citrus and sweet fig, paired with a cake-like base and light crumble topping...it really doesn't get much better than this!

INGREDIENTS

Base/Crumble Layer

- 2 cups almond flour
- ¼ cup ground flaxseed
- 1 cup medjool dates
- 1 teaspoon vanilla extract
- dash of salt
- 1 teaspoon water (if needed)

Filling Layer

- 2 cups soaked figs (soaked for 2 hours in warm water)
- ½ cup Date Paste (see Essentials)
- 1 fresh lemon, juiced
- 4 teaspoons orange zest

HOW TO MAKE

Base/Crumble Layer

Process all ingredients in the food processor until well combined and crumbly in texture. Press ¾ of the mixture into a parchment-lined 4x4 inch pan. Set aside remaining mixture.

Filling Layer

Blend all ingredients in a blender until well combined and smooth. Spread filling evenly onto crust. Sprinkle remaining base layer mixture on top of filling and lightly cover. Place in the refrigerator or freezer and let set for 1 hour. Serve and enjoy. Uneaten dessert can be stored in the refrigerator for up to 1 week or in the freezer for up to 1 month.

Helpful Hints

To make serving these bars easier, cut while frozen. After cutting, allow them to sit at room temperature for 30 minutes before serving.

CHAPTER 3

CAKES & TARTS

Strawberry Cheesecake

If you are looking for the perfect crowd-pleasing dessert, then this is all you will need. Fresh, light and creamy, this heavenly Strawberry Cheesecake is great for any spring or summer dinner party!

INGREDIENTS

Crust

- 1 cup almonds
- 6 deglet noor dates
- ¼ teaspoon cinnamon
- dash of salt

Filling

- 2 cups raw cashews (soaked for 2 hours)
- 8 medjool dates
- ⅔ cup refined coconut oil, melted
- 2 teaspoons vanilla extract
- 2 tablespoons lemon juice
- ¼ cup cherries (for color)
- 2 cups strawberries

HOW TO MAKE

Crust

Process all ingredients until you achieve a graham cracker-like consistency in the food processor. Firmly press this mixture into the base of 2 small springform pans or 12 mini silicone molds. Set aside.

Filling

Process all ingredients (excluding strawberries) until evenly blended in the food processor. Add strawberries and process into a smooth and creamy consistency. Evenly spread the filling on the top of the base crust. Place finished cheesecake in freezer for 4 hours. Uneaten dessert can be stored in the freezer for up to 1 month.

 ## Helpful Hints

If you are unable to use fresh fruit, be sure to fully thaw your strawberries before adding them into the filling; otherwise the coconut oil will harden up and create a chunky looking texture.

SOAK

PREP

FREEZE

2 *hrs*

15 *min*

4 *hrs*

Chocolate Espresso Tart

Sometimes, convincing people that a treat made with no refined sugar can actually taste delicious feels like an impossible mission. But once the doubters taste this sinful blend of chocolate and espresso, they will all beg you for the recipe!

INGREDIENTS

Crust

- 1 cup walnuts
- ½ cup deglet noor dates
- 2 tablespoons cacao powder
- ¼ teaspoon cinnamon
- dash of salt

Filling

- 2 cup raw cashews (soaked for 2 hours)
- ¾ cup Date Paste (see Essentials)
- 4 tablespoons refined coconut oil, melted
- 2 teaspoon vanilla extract
- 3 tablespoons cacao powder
- ⅔ cup Cold Brew Coffee (see Essentials)

Topping

- Vanilla Whipped Cream (see Essentials)

HOW TO MAKE

Crust

Process all ingredients until you see a graham cracker-like consistency in the food processor. Firmly press the crust mixture into the base of two small tart pans. Set aside.

Filling

Process the soaked cashews for about 1 minute in the food processor. Add all the remaining ingredients until the filling has a smooth, even consistency. Evenly spread the filling onto the base crust. Set in the freezer for 4 hours.

Topping

Top with Vanilla Whipped Cream (optional). Serve and enjoy. Uneaten dessert can be stored in the refrigerator for up to 1 week or in the freezer for up to 1 month.

 ## Helpful Hints

To make these tarts over the top cute, think a little outside the box by making them in mini coffee cups. Mini desserts are the trend right now and this presentation will make the dessert the highlight of any dinner party or event.

SOAK   PREP   FREEZE

2 *hrs*   20 *min*   4 *hrs*

Pina Colada Cheesecake

"If you like pina coladas, gettin' caught in the rain..." I am so tone deaf it isn't even funny, but every time I make this recipe I am singing this song out loud. This cheesecake is fun, tropical and fruity. With only a small hint of coconut, but a big burst of pineapple flavor this dessert can be served year round at your house.

INGREDIENTS

Crust

- ¾ cup macadamia nuts
- ½ cup unsweetened shredded coconut
- ½ cup deglet noor dates
- 1 teaspoon cinnamon
- ½ teaspoon vanilla extract
- dash of salt

Filling

- 2 cups raw cashews (soaked for 2 hours)
- 12 medjool dates
- ½ cup refined coconut oil, melted
- ¾ cup coconut cream
- 1 teaspoon vanilla extract
- 1 cup pineapple (blended)

Glaze

- 1 cup pineapple chunks
- 1 tablespoon refined coconut oil, melted

HOW TO MAKE

Crust

Process all ingredients until there is a chunky, graham cracker-like consistency in the food processor. Firmly press crust mixture into the base of 2 small springform pans or 12 mini silicone molds. Set aside.

Filling

Process all ingredients into a smooth, even consistency in the food processor. Evenly spread filling onto crust base. Set aside in the freezer.

Glaze

Blend all ingredients in a blender until smooth. Evenly spread onto filling. Freeze for 4 hours. Uneaten dessert can be stored in the refrigerator for up to 1 week or in the freezer for up to 1 month.

 ### Helpful Hints

I know pineapple isn't always in season, so simply thaw a bag of organic frozen pineapple!

Bite-Size Black Forest Cakes

Every dessert cookbook needs a chocolate cake recipe, right? Well this cake recipe is very special to me because it was my Grammy Vigneault's favorite! This Black Forest Cake recipe is one part moist & rich and one part light & airy! And the pairing with the Vanilla Whipped Cream recipe is pure PERFECTION!

INGREDIENTS

Cake

- 1 ½ cup hazelnuts
- ½ cup walnuts
- 2 cups medjool dates
- ⅓ cup dried bing cherries
- 1 cup cacao powder
- 2 teaspoons vanilla extract
- dash of salt

Frosting

- Vanilla Whipped Cream recipe (see Essentials)
- 20-24 thawed bing cherries

HOW TO MAKE

Cake

Process all dry ingredients until flour-like in consistency in the food processor. Add remaining ingredients and process until an even consistency. The mixture should turn into a dough ball. Firmly press cake mixture into a mini cupcake silicone mold and refrigerate for 1 hour.

Frosting

Remove cake from silicone mold. Add Vanilla Whipped Cream and top with a cherry on each mini cake. Uneaten dessert can be stored in the refrigerator for up to 1 week.

Helpful Hints

If possible, don't top your cake with whipped cream until ready to serve. If that isn't an option, be sure to keep in the refrigerator until ready to eat as the cream will lose it form.

Blueberry Cheesecake

Blueberry Cheesecake was the very first cheesecake recipe I ever created, and although it took me close to 10 attempts to lock it in, I can truly say that this method inspired all of the other cheesecakes in this book. Oh, and did I mention that it is so good my 2-year-old nephew asks for it by name! "Auntie Wawa, Blue Cake Peeeez." The best part is I don't have to feel guilty about giving it to him!

INGREDIENTS

Crust

- 1 cup almonds
- 6 deglet noor dates
- dash of salt
- ¼ teaspoon cinnamon

Filling

- 2 cups raw cashews (soaked for 2 hours)
- 8 medjool dates
- ⅔ cup refined coconut oil, melted
- 2 teaspoon vanilla extract
- 3 tablespoons lemon juice
- 2 cups blueberries

Glaze

- 1 cup blueberries
- 2 medjool dates
- 1 tablespoon refined coconut oil, melted

HOW TO MAKE

Crust

Process all ingredients until graham cracker-like consistency in the food processor. Firmly press crust mixture into the base of 2 small springform or 12 mini silicone molds. Set aside.

Filling

Process all ingredients into a smooth, even consistency in the food processor. Evenly spread the filling onto the base. Set aside in the freezer.

Glaze

Process all ingredients (excluding blueberries) until evenly blended in the food processor. Add blueberries and process into a smooth and creamy consistency. Evenly spread the filling on the top of the base crust. Place in freezer.

 ## Helpful Hints

This recipe is good with, or without, the glaze. If you are making a large cheesecake, I suggest putting on the glaze right before serving to prevent the top layer from running down the sides of the cake. This happens as the cheesecake thaws.

Apple Crumble

I LOVE apple crumble, but all of the traditional recipes call for a large amount of sugar and butter. All of the raw versions already out there were either smothered in maple syrup or agave. So, I made it my personal goal to create a healthy version that would taste just as good without the crazy blood sugar spike! Now you can pig out on this delicious dessert at your next barbeque or picnic with no guilt!

INGREDIENTS

Crust

- ½ cup walnuts
- 1 ¼ cup pecans
- ½ cup deglet noor dates

Apple Sauce

- 2 green apples (peeled and cut into small chunks)
- ½ cup deglet noor
- dates
- 2 teaspoons cinnamon
- ¼ cup raisins

Apple Filling

- 2 green apples (peeled and sliced)

HOW TO MAKE

Crust

Process all ingredients in a food processor until you achieve a graham cracker-like consistency. Press ¾ of the mixture into a parchment lined 4x4 inch pan or mini springform pan. Set aside remaining crust mixture.

Apple Sauce

Process all ingredients until a smooth, even consistency in the food processor. Place sauce into medium mixing bowl.

Apple Filling

Fold apple slices into applesauce and evenly spread filling onto crust. Sprinkle the remaining crust mixture on top. Refrigerate for 2 hours. Uneaten dessert can be stored in the refrigerator for up to 1 week.

 ## Helpful Hints

Make the base a thin, but firm, even layer, about ¼ of an inch thick. This will help make sure that the cinnamon apples are the super star, not the pecans.

Pumpkin Cheesecake

Thanksgiving has always been one of my favorite holidays because of the great family time it brings. Because of this, I wanted to make a healthy gourmet-style Pumpkin Cheesecake that the whole family could enjoy. I am happy to say that my family has now replaced our traditional homemade pumpkin pie with this flavor-packed seasonal cheesecake.

INGREDIENTS

Crust

- 2 cups pecans
- 20 deglet noor dates
- dash of salt

Filling

- 2 cups raw cashews (soaked for 2 hours)
- 1 ½ cups pumpkin puree
- ½ cup chopped carrot
- 1 cup medjool dates
- ½ cup refined, coconut oil, melted
- 2 tablespoons vanilla extract
- 4 teaspoons cinnamon
- ½ teaspoon nutmeg

HOW TO MAKE

Crust

Process all ingredients until a graham cracker-like consistency in the food processor. Firmly press crust mixture into the base of 2 small springform pans or 12 mini silicone molds. Set aside.

Filling

Process all ingredients until a smooth, even consistency in the food processor. Evenly spread filling over base crust. Set aside in the freezer for 4 hours. Uneaten dessert can be stored in the refrigerator for up to 1 week or in the freezer for up to 1 month.

 ## Helpful Hints

If the holidays get as crazy for you as they do for me, you can make this cheesecake up to 1 month early! Store it in the freezer and allow it to thaw in the refrigerator for 24 hours before serving.

Fruit Tart

This Fruit Tart will make a beautiful addition to any spring or summer event! With its graham cracker-like crust and a light, sweet citrus custard filling, it will be hard to share!

INGREDIENTS

Crust

- 1 cup almonds
- ½ cup deglet noor dates
- 1 teaspoon cinnamon
- dash of salt

Filling

- 2 cups raw cashews (soaked for at least 2 hours, or overnight)
- ⅓ cup sweet almond milk (see Essentials)
- 3 tablespoons Date Paste (see Essentials)
- I teaspoon refined coconut oil, melted
- 1 teaspoon vanilla extract
- 1 lemon, juiced
- 1 large orange, juiced
- pinch of salt
- 1 cup mixed fruit (for garnishing)

HOW TO MAKE

Crust

Process all ingredients until a graham cracker-like consistency in the food processor. Firmly press crust mixture into the base of 2 small tart pans. Set aside.

Filling

Process cashews for about 1 minute in the food processor. Add all remaining ingredients until a smooth, even consistency. If it is still not smooth enough, then transfer the mixture to a blender for 1 additional minute. Evenly spread the filling onto the crust base. Set aside in the freezer for 1 hour. Top with fruit of choice before serving. Serve and enjoy. Uneaten dessert can be stored in the refrigerator for up to 1 week.

 ## Helpful Hints

Using a tart tamper will ensure a perfectly shaped crust every time.

Chocolate Raspberry Cheesecake

Calling all chocolate and raspberry lovers! I cannot express my love for this dessert enough. If you love a rich and sweet dessert, say hello to your new best friend!

INGREDIENTS

Crust

- ½ cup walnuts
- 3 deglet noor dates
- dash of salt
- 1 teaspoon cacao powder
- pinch of cinnamon

Filling

- 2 cups raw cashews (soaked for 2 hours)
- 6 medjool dates
- ½ cup cacao powder
- ¼ cup refined coconut oil, melted
- 1 teaspoon vanilla extract
- 2 tablespoons Sweet Cashew Milk (see Essentials)
- 2 cups raspberries (juiced)
- pinch of salt

Glaze

- 1 cup raspberries
- 1 tablespoon refined coconut oil, melted

HOW TO MAKE

Crust

Process all ingredients until a graham cracker-like consistency in the food processor. Firmly press crust into the base of 2 mini springform pans or 12 mini silicone molds. Set aside.

Filling

Process all ingredients until a smooth, even consistency in the food processor. Evenly spread filling onto base. Set aside in the freezer while you make the glaze. Leftovers can be stored in the refrigerator for up to 1 week or in the freezer for up to one month.

Glaze

Blend all ingredients in a blender. Evenly spread on top of the filling. Freeze for 4 hours. Uneaten dessert can be stored in the refrigerator for up to 1 week or in the freezer for up to 1 month.

 ## Helpful Hints

Straining the raspberry seeds is a MUST. Otherwise, you will end up chewing on the raspberry seeds.

Bananas Foster Tart

This Bananas Foster Tart is simply stunning. With a thick and creamy banana-infused filling and smooth caramel topping, it's mouth-watering good!

INGREDIENTS

Crust

- ½ cup almonds
- ½ cup walnuts
- 10 deglet noor dates
- dash of salt
- ½ teaspoon cinnamon

Filling

- 2 cups raw cashews (soaked for 2 hours)
- ¾ cup medjool dates
- 1/3 cup refined coconut oil, melted
- 1 teaspoon vanilla extract
- 2 vanilla bean pods (scraped)
- 1 lemon, juiced
- ½ cup coconut milk
- 2 bananas (ripe to slightly over-ripe)

Glaze

- Date Paste (see Essentials)
- 1 cup sliced bananas

HOW TO MAKE

Crust

Process all ingredients until a graham cracker-like consistency in the food processor. Firmly press crust into the base of 2 small springform pans or 12 mini silicone molds. Set aside.

Filling

Process all ingredients until a smooth, even consistency in the food processor. Evenly spread filling onto base. Set aside in the freezer for 4 hours.

Glaze

See Date Paste recipe. Spread date paste over the filling. Add sliced bananas on top as a garnish. Uneaten dessert can be stored in the refrigerator for up to 1 week or in the freezer for up to 1 month.

 ### Helpful Hints

To avoid brown bananas don't garnish your cake until you are ready to serve.

CHAPTER 4

CANDIES, FUDGE & TRUFFLES

Peanut Butter Cups

Peanut butter and chocolate—this is the holy grail of flavor combinations. Chocolaty, nutty, melt-in-your-mouth yumminess! This is my husband's favorite recipe in the whole book! I make a fresh batch every single week.

INGREDIENTS

Chocolate

- ¼ cup refined coconut oil, melted
- ½ teaspoon vanilla extract
- 3 tablespoons yacon syrup
- ¼ cup cacao powder
- (18-24) mini cupcake wrappers

Peanut Butter Filling

- ½ cup natural peanut butter
- 2 tablespoons refined coconut oil, melted
- ½ teaspoon vanilla extract
- 1 tablespoon Date Paste (see Essentials)

HOW TO MAKE

Chocolate

Mix all wet ingredients together in a small mixing bowl. Add cacao powder and whisk until well blended. Use a measuring spoon to distribute ½ teaspoon of the chocolate mixture into each mini cupcake wrapper. Place on a tray and then transport into the freezer.

Peanut Butter Filling

Mix all ingredients together in a small mixing bowl until well blended. Measure out 1 teaspoon of peanut butter filling onto each base chocolate layer. Place in the freezer to set for 15 minutes. Top peanut butter filling with ½-1 teaspoon of the remaining chocolate mixture to finish off these perfect little candies. Freeze for 10 minutes. Extras can be stored in the freezer for up to 1 month.

 ## Helpful Hints

A little bit goes a long way with the chocolate sauce. Let the peanut butter be the star of these candies. Peanut Butter Cups are best enjoyed straight from the freezer.

Espresso Truffles

Just the thought of espresso and chocolate puts a smile on my face. It is the perfect treat to complement a cup of coffee or to satisfy your sweet tooth at the end of a long day! These truffles are rich, sweet and delicious.

INGREDIENTS

Truffles Base

- 1 cup hazelnuts
- 1 teaspoon organic ground coffee
- 3 tablespoons Cold Brew Coffee (see Essentials)
- 1 cup cacao powder
- ⅛ teaspoon salt
- ½ teaspoon cinnamon
- 12 medjool dates
- 1 teaspoon vanilla extract
- 1 medium ripe avocado

Chocolate

- ¼ cup refined coconut oil, melted
- ½ teaspoon vanilla extract
- 3 tablespoons yacon syrup
- ¼ cup cacao powder

HOW TO MAKE

Truffles Base

Process all dry ingredients together until flour-like in consistency in the food processor. Add pitted dates and process until the mixture is an even, crumbly consistency. Add the remaining ingredients and process until the dough turns into ball. Roll the dough into 1 inch balls, place on plate and put into the refrigerator while making the chocolate coating.

Chocolate

Mix all wet ingredients together in a small mixing bowl. Add cacao powder and whisk until well blended. Dip truffles base into the chocolate with a fork and place onto cookie sheet lined with parchment paper. Place in the refrigerator for 10 minutes, serve and enjoy. Extras can be stored in the refrigerator for up to 1 week.

 Helpful Hints

I used to top these delicious balls of yumminess with a whole coffee bean, but I found people were trying to eat them. I now garnish the truffles with ground coffee and then sprinkle coffee beans on the plate for presentation.

Coconut Bites

If you like Almond Joy or Mounds, you are going to love my healthy version! They are quick and easy to make and will make you feel like a little kid again!

INGREDIENTS

Coconut Filling

- 1 ¼ cup unsweetened shredded coconut
- 1 tablespoon refined coconut oil, melted
- 1 tablespoon Date Paste (see Essentials)

Chocolate Coating

- ¼ cup refined coconut oil, melted
- ½ teaspoon vanilla extract
- 3 tablespoons yacon syrup
- ¼ cup cacao powder

HOW TO MAKE

Coconut Filling

Process all ingredients together until the filling has an even, chunky consistency in the food processor. Press the filling mixture into mini square silicone mold. Place in the freezer for 20 minutes.

Chocolate Coating

Mix all wet ingredients together in a small mixing bowl. Add cacao powder and whisk until well blended. Remove coconut filling from the mold. Dip each piece of coconut filling into the chocolate and place onto a parchment paper lined plate. Place in the refrigerator for 10 minutes, serve and enjoy. Extras can be stored in the freezer for up to 1 month.

 Helpful Hints

These are best enjoyed frozen. If you want to perfectly recreate an Almond Joy, simply place an almond on top of the coconut filling before submerging in chocolate.

Chocolate Fudge

Chocolate fudge! Do I really need to say more? Just minutes after the photo shoot, my husband and photographer ate every last morsel of fudge. Thank goodness we didn't need a backup shot!

INGREDIENTS

- ⅓ cup hazelnuts
- ½ cup cacao powder
- ¼ cup refined coconut oil, melted
- ¾ cup Date Paste (see Essentials)
- 1 teaspoon vanilla extract
- ½ cup chopped walnuts (optional)

HOW TO MAKE

Process all dry ingredients together until a flour-like consistency in the food processor. Add remaining ingredients and process until there is an even, smooth consistency. Add chopped walnuts if desired. Place into a 4x4 inch pan lined with parchment paper. Freeze for 2 hours. Cut into small squares pieces, serve and enjoy. Extras can be stored in the refrigerator for up to 1 week or the freezer for up to one month.

Helpful Hints

I cut these while still frozen to create the perfect square bites.

Chocolate Bar

This recipe was created for those moments when you just need a little something...I am not going to lie, chocolate does make everything taste better! That's why I created a healthy version that you won't have to feel guilty about!

INGREDIENTS

Chocolate

- ¼ cup refined coconut oil, melted
- ½ teaspoon vanilla extract
- 2 ½ tablespoons yacon syrup
- ¼ cup cacao powder

HOW TO MAKE

Mix all wet ingredients together in a small mixing bowl. Add cacao powder and whisk until well blended. Pour the chocolate into a fun chocolate bar mold or a 4x4 inch pan lined with parchment paper. Freeze for 20 minutes. Enjoy! Extra can be stored in the freezer for up to 1 month.

Helpful Hints

Keep your chocolate bar frozen until you are ready to eat so it won't melt too quickly.

Peppermint Bites

If you like peppermint patties or thin mints you can start jumping for joy right now!! These bites have just the right amount of peppermint filling and sweet chocolate coating to make your tongue do a happy dance.

INGREDIENTS

Mint Filling

- ¼ cup raw cashews
- ¼ cup refined coconut oil, melted
- ⅛ cup coconut butter (warmed & mixed)
- 2 drops food-grade peppermint oil
- ½ teaspoon vanilla extract
- pinch of salt

Chocolate Coating

- ¼ cup refined coconut oil, melted
- ½ teaspoon vanilla extract
- 3 tablespoons yacon syrup
- ¼ cup cacao powder

HOW TO MAKE

Mint Filling

Process cashews until a flour-like consistency in the food processor. Add all remaining ingredients and process until it is an even, smooth consistency. Pour filling mixture into a mini circular silicone mold. Place in the freezer for 20 minutes.

Chocolate Coating

Mix all wet ingredients together in a small mixing bowl. Add cacao powder and whisk until well blended. Remove mint fillings from the mold. Dip each individual candy into chocolate and place onto parchment paper. Place in the refrigerator for 10 minutes, serve and enjoy. Extras can be stored in the freezer for up to 1month.

Helpful Hints

These should be served frozen for the perfect texture and to avoid a mess...unless you plan on just licking delicious chocolate and mint filling off your hands.

Chocolate Truffles

This was the very first truffle recipe I ever made! It holds a very special place in my heart as I spent hours trying to create the perfect filling that would be rich and smooth enough to satisfy even the most sinful chocolate lover's taste buds! The time and energy paid off as this is the #1 request I receive for dessert orders! These chocolate truffles are pretty enough to take to any dinner party, but also easy enough to make at home any night of the week.

INGREDIENTS

Truffle Base

- 1 cup hazelnuts
- 1 cup cacao powder
- ⅛ teaspoon salt
- 1 teaspoon vanilla extract
- 12 medjool dates
- ¼ cup dried bing cherries
- 1 medium ripe avocado

Chocolate

- ¼ cup refined coconut oil, melted
- ½ teaspoon vanilla extract
- 3 tablespoons yacon syrup
- ¼ cup cacao powder

HOW TO MAKE

Truffle Base

Process all dry ingredients together until a flour-like consistency in the food processor. Add pitted dates and cherries. Process until dough turns into ball.

Add remaining ingredients and process until an even consistency.

Roll into bite-size balls.

Chocolate

Mix all wet ingredients together in a small mixing bowl. Add cacao powder and whisk until well blended. Dip truffles into chocolate with a fork and place onto a plate lined with parchment paper. Place in the refrigerator for 10 minutes, serve and enjoy. Extras can be stored in the refrigerator for up to 1 week.

Helpful Hints

To make the truffles look smooth and perfect, refrigerate the truffle filling for an additional 20 minutes after shaping them into balls. Then dunk into your fresh chocolate sauce, place on parchment paper and top with your choice of goji berries, peanut butter drizzle or any other fun combos you can come up with!

Peanut Butter Fudge

WARNING: IF YOU DO NOT LIKE PEANUT BUTTER, DO NOT MAKE THIS RECIPE! IT WILL SEND YOUR TASTE BUDS INTO PEANUT BUTTER OVERLOAD!!! I simply love how delicious and easy this recipe is! With only two ingredients, this is my go-to recipe when unexpected friends stop in to say hello.

INGREDIENTS

- 12 medjool dates
- 1 cup natural peanut butter

HOW TO MAKE

Process all ingredients in the food processor until the dough turns into ball. Press the mixture firmly into a pan lined with parchment paper firmly. Freeze for 2 hours. Cut into squares. Serve and enjoy. Extras can be stored in the refrigerator for up to 1 week or the freezer 1 month.

Helpful Hints

Cut your fudge while it is still frozen, but then allow it to sit in your refrigerator for up to 3 hours before serving for the best appearance and texture.

Peanut & Caramel Chocolate Bites

With a cookie-like crust, layered with caramel and peanuts, then coated in chocolate, all I can say is YUMMY!!! I created this recipe for a friend who desperately missed the original Snickers candy she used to eat in her teens. Seeing the smile on her face when she tried this for the first time was more than worth the time it took to create!

INGREDIENTS

Base

- 1 cup almonds
- 1 cup cashews
- ¼ cup Date Paste (see Essentials)
- 1 tablespoon refined coconut oil, melted
- dash of salt

Caramel

- 1 cup medjool dates
- 2 tablespoons natural peanut butter
- ⅓ cup peanuts

Chocolate

- ¼ cup refined coconut oil, melted
- ½ teaspoon vanilla extract
- 3 tablespoons yacon syrup
- ¼ cup cacao powder

HOW TO MAKE

Base

Process almonds and cashews until a flour-like consistency in the food processor. Add all remaining ingredients and process until even in consistency. Press base into a silicone mini square mold. Place in the freezer for 20 minutes.

Caramel

Process dates and peanut butter in the food processor until you see a smooth, sticky consistency. Add peanuts and pulse until evenly blended. Press the caramel mixture into base in silicone mold. Place back in the freezer for 20 minutes.

Chocolate

Mix all wet ingredients together in a small mixing bowl. Add cacao powder and whisk until well blended. Remove the candies from the mold. Dip each candy into chocolate and place onto a plate lined with parchment paper. Place in the refrigerator for 10 minutes, then serve and enjoy. Extras can be stored in the freezer for 1 month.

 Helpful Hints

The caramel can get sticky. I suggest letting it set in the refrigerator for up to 10 minutes before spreading it onto the base to allow for easier handling.

Citrus Truffles

I love these orange-infused truffles!! The sweet orange flavor brings out the rich and heavenly chocolate flavors! It is impossible to eat just one.

INGREDIENTS

Truffle Base

- 1 cup hazelnuts
- 1 cup cacao powder
- ⅛ teaspoon salt
- 1 teaspoon vanilla extract
- 12 medjool dates
- 1 medium ripe avocado
- 2 teaspoons orange juice
- 2 teaspoons orange zest

Chocolate

- ¼ cup refined coconut oil, melted
- ½ teaspoon vanilla extract
- 3 tablespoons yacon syrup
- ¼ cup cacao powder

HOW TO MAKE

Truffle Base

Process all dry ingredients together until a flour-like consistency in the food processor. Add pitted dates and process until even in consistency. Add remaining ingredients into the food processor and process until the dough turns into ball. Roll the dough into 1 inch balls.

Chocolate

Mix all wet ingredients together in a small mixing bowl. Add cacao powder and whisk until well blended. Dip truffle center into chocolate with a fork and place onto parchment paper. Place in the refrigerator for 10 minutes, serve and enjoy. Extras can be stored in the refrigerator for up to 1 week.

Helpful Hints

Use a zester instead of a grater for perfect zest. A zester creates thin, long, and curly orange peels that are better for decorating.

CHAPTER 5

FROZEN TREATS, ICE CREAM & SORBET

Strawberry Ice Cream

This beautiful, smooth ice cream has a light fruit flavor that will bring you back to the days when you would chase the ice cream truck for your favorite treat!

INGREDIENTS

- 3 cups strawberries
- 1 cup raw cashews (soaked for 2 hours)
- 1 cup Sweet Cashew Milk (see Essentials)
- ¼ cup refined coconut oil, melted
- 2 tablespoons vanilla extract
- ¼ cup bing cherries (for color)
- dash of salt

HOW TO MAKE

Blend all ingredients except for coconut oil in the blender until smooth and creamy. Add coconut oil and blend thoroughly. Pour into an ice cream maker and follow the manufacturer's instructions. Once your soft serve is ready, fold in a cup of chopped strawberries.

Helpful Hints

This is best served fresh out of your ice cream maker. For a little extra yumminess, add some fresh chocolate sauce!

Chocolate Fudge Popsicles

For all of my chocolate lovers out there...this one's for you! These pops are something that both adults and children will love!

INGREDIENTS

- 1 cup raw cashews (soaked for 2 hours)
- 2 cups Sweet Almond Milk (see Essentials)
- ½ cup coconut butter, melted
- ½ cup refined coconut oil, melted
- 1 tablespoon vanilla extract
- ¾ cup Date Paste (see Essentials)
- ¾ cup cacao powder
- dash of salt

HOW TO MAKE

Blend all ingredients in the blender until smooth and creamy. Pour into 12 pop molds. Freeze overnight. Enjoy.

Helpful Hints

To remove popsicle from mold, simply run under warm water and then pull. It will guarantee a perfect pop every time! And if you really like chocolate, add an additional tablespoon of cacao powder.

Mango Sorbet

I may or may not be eating this very dessert as I am writing the description! I keep a container of this ready to eat at all times because you never know when an urge to eat delicious fruity sorbet will hit!

INGREDIENTS

- 4 cups mango
- ½ cup Date Paste (see Essentials)
- 2 tablespoons lemon juice

HOW TO MAKE

Blend all ingredients in the blender until smooth and creamy. Pour into an ice cream maker and follow the manufacturer's instructions for sorbet.

 Helpful Hints

If you are storing in the freezer, place the sorbet into a sorbet or ice cream container once the recipe is complete. Allow 5-10 minutes for it to soften naturally before serving, otherwise you could bend a spoon or two.

PREP   **FREEZE**

5 min   *3 hrs*

Strawberry Bars

These are the healthiest, cleanest and most refreshing strawberry bars out there. During warm summer nights, these are all you will need.

INGREDIENTS

- 2 cups of strawberries

- 1 tablespoon of Date Paste (see Essentials)

- 1 teaspoon of lemon juice

HOW TO MAKE

Blend all ingredients in the blender until smooth. Pour the mixture into 6 freezer pop molds. Freeze overnight.

 Helpful Hints

Add a handful of chopped strawberries into each mold before you freeze them for extra fruitiness in each bite!

Green Tea Ice Cream

Dear sophisticated dessert lover, this one's for you!

INGREDIENTS

- 2 frozen bananas (slice into coins before freezing)
- 2 teaspoons matcha green tea powder
- 1 cup Sweet Cashew Milk (see Essentials)

HOW TO MAKE

Blend all ingredients in the blender until smooth. Pour the mixture into an ice cream maker and follow the manufacturer's instructions.

Helpful Hints

If you would like it to be even sweeter, add a tablespoon of Date Paste.

Mango Cherry Popsicles

These pops were made 100% for my little nephew! He LOVES pops and it is impossible to find healthy popsicles in the store. Now, I always have at least one or two Mango Cherry Popsicles ready when he comes. You can now ditch those sugary, store-bought popsicles!

INGREDIENTS

Mango Layer

- 3 cups mango chunks
- 1 tablespoon Date Paste (see Essentials)
- 1 cup water

Cherry Layer

- Remaining Mango Layer mixture
- 1 cup cherries

HOW TO MAKE

Mango Layer

Blend all ingredients in the blender until smooth. Pour half of the mixture into 6 freezer pop molds, leaving the remaining room for the cherry layer.

Cherry Layer

Blend all ingredients in the blender until smooth. Pour into the freezer pop molds on top of the first mango layer. Freeze overnight.

Helpful Hints

You can really use any flavors or molds you want, but make them fun for the little ones!

SOAK   PREP   FREEZE

2 *hrs*   10 *min*   1 *hr*

Chocolate Ice Cream

No fancy ingredients here, just a simple, rich and creamy chocolate flavor with a silky, smooth ice cream texture. It's like a frozen chocolate mousse!

INGREDIENTS

- 1 ½ cup cashews (soaked for 2 hours)
- 1 ¾ cup Sweet Cashew Milk (see Essentials)
- 5 tablespoons cacao powder
- 2 tablespoons vanilla extract
- 6 tablespoons Date Paste (see Essentials)
- 3 tablespoons refined coconut oil, melted
- dash of salt

HOW TO MAKE

Blend all ingredients, except for coconut oil, in the blender until smooth. Add coconut oil and blend thoroughly. Pour into ice cream maker and follow the manufacturer's instructions for an ice cream.

 Helpful Hints

Ok, this is a little overindulgent, but so good! My husband crushed up the Peanut Butter Cups to add in the ice cream and then topped it with the Chocolate Sauce!! It is chocolaty paradise!

Freezer Pops

Sometimes we all just want a quick, cool, refreshing pop. They bring us back to a simpler time! Here are two of my favorite tried-and-true recipes.

INGREDIENTS

Strawberries & Cream

- ¼ cup coconut milk
- 1 ½ cup strawberries
- 1 tablespoon Date Paste (see Essentials)
- ½ teaspoon vanilla extract
- ½ teaspoon water

Tropical Blast

- 1 cup pineapple
- 1 cup mango
- 1 cup banana

HOW TO MAKE

Strawberries & Cream

Blend all the ingredients in the blender until smooth. Pour into 6 freezer pop molds or about 18 popsicle pouches. Freeze overnight.

Tropical Blast

Blend all the ingredients in the blender until smooth. Pour into 6 freezer pop molds or about 18 popsicle pouches. Freeze overnight.

Helpful Hints

These don't have to be placed into popsicle pouches, but it sure does make them even cuter!

Raspberry Sorbet

Raspberry sorbet is quite possibly the most popular of all the sorbet flavors. It is the perfect light summer treat with its refreshing sweet-tart flavor.

INGREDIENTS

- 4 cups raspberries
- ¼ cup Date Paste (see Essentials)
- 1 banana

HOW TO MAKE

Blend all ingredients in the blender until smooth. Pour into an ice cream maker and follow the manufacturer's instructions for sorbet.

Helpful Hints

For an extra smooth sorbet, use a small mesh strainer to deseed the raspberry puree.

Orange Tropical Bliss Bars

Not sure what to make your kids for a healthy treat on a warm day? Well this recipe only has 3 ingredients and takes less than 5 minutes to make before popping in the freezer to harden. The best part is that if you make these in the morning they will be ready after a day of fun events!

INGREDIENTS

- 1 banana
- 1 orange
- 1 cup pineapple

HOW TO MAKE

Blend all ingredients in blender until smooth. Pour into 6 pop molds. Freeze 3 hours.

Helpful Hints

Use fresh ingredients for the best flavor! If you don't have those available, add about 1 cup of water to help with blending frozen fruit.

HOW TO CONTACT
NATURALLY HEALTHY DESSERTS

f /naturallyhealthydesserts

🐦 @healthymarquis

P /healthymarquis

📷 @naturallyhealthydesserts

Thank you so much

FOR JOINING THE NATURALLY HEALTHY LIFESTYLE!

I would love to see your creations! Please tag me and use #NaturallyHealthy when you post your photos.

For more recipes and videos, visit NaturallyHealthyDesserts.com.

Host your very own Naturally Healthy Dessert Workshop or Event by emailing me at: Laura@naturallyhealthymarquis.com.

hand crafted
NATURALLY HEALTHY
Est DESSERTS 2015
· organic ·

Index